Lerner *SPORTS*

SUPER SPORTS TEAMS

INSIDE THE
GOLDEN STATE
WARRIORS

DAVID STABLER

Lerner Publications ◆ Minneapolis

SPORTS THRILLS *MEET* RESEARCH SKILLS

Lerner SPORTS

Free Database Trial: **lernersports.com**

Lerner Publications Company
An imprint of Lerner Publishing Group, Inc.
241 First Avenue North
Minneapolis, MN 55401 USA

For reading levels and more information, look up this title at www.lernerbooks.com.

Main body text set in Aptifer Slab LT Pro / Typeface provided by Linotype AG

Library of Congress Cataloging-in-Publication Data

Names: Stabler, David, author.
Title: Inside the Golden State Warriors / by David Stabler.
Description: Minneapolis : Lerner Publications, 2023. | Series: Super sports teams. Lerner sports | Includes
    bibliographical references and index. | Audience: Ages 7–11 | Audience: Grades 4–6 | Summary: "Since 19
    Golden State Warriors have been making basketball history. Relive their greatest moments, explore ho
    team has adapted through difficult seasons, and learn about star players like Steph Curry, Kevin Dura
    Wilt Chamberlain"— Provided by publisher.
Identifiers: LCCN 2022007922 (print) | LCCN 2022007923 (ebook) | ISBN 9781728476087 (library binding) |
    ISBN 9781728478661 (paperback) | ISBN 9781728485140 (ebook)
Subjects: LCSH: Golden State Warriors (Basketball team)—History—Juvenile literature.
Classification: LCC GV885.52.G64 S73 2023 (print) | LCC GV885.52.G64 (ebook) | DDC 796.323/640979461—dc
    eng/20220322

LC record available at https://lccn.loc.gov/2022007922
LC ebook record available at https://lccn.loc.gov/2022007923

Manufactured in the United States of America

TABLE OF CONTENTS

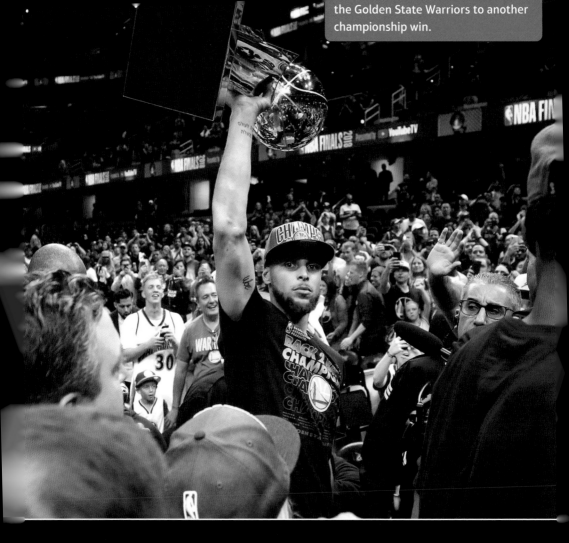

the Golden State Warriors to another championship win.

CHAMPIONS AGAIN

- From 1946 to 1962, the Warriors played in **PHILADELPHIA, PENNSYLVANIA**.

- The Warriors have 19 players and coaches in the **BASKETBALL HALL OF FAME**.

- The **WARRIORS** won back-to-back National Basketball Association (NBA) titles in 2017 and 2018.

- The Warriors have won seven NBA **CHAMPIONSHIPS**.

The Golden State Warriors faced the Cleveland Cavaliers in the 2018 NBA Finals. It was the fourth year in a row the two teams had faced each other in the Finals. Superstar LeBron James led the Cavaliers. James and his teammates were hoping to win their second championship. The Warriors had other ideas. But Golden State had lost 10 of their final 17 regular season games. Some thought the Cavaliers might have the advantage this year.

The Warriors started with an overtime win in Game 1. Forward Kevin Durant led the way with 38 points. Guard Stephen Curry helped with 28 points. The Warriors beat the Cavaliers in Games 2, 3, and 4 to take the series in a four-game sweep. Curry scored 37 points

three-point shots. Durant added 20 points, 12 rebounds, and 10 assists for a
rare triple-double. He won the Finals Most Valuable Player (MVP) award.

The victory was the Warriors' third NBA title in four years. Before 2015,
the team hadn't won a title since 1975.

Even legendary LeBron James (*left*) was no match for Klay Thompson (*right*) and the Golden State Warriors in the 2018 NBA Finals.

Kevin Durant helped the Warriors make it to the NBA Finals all three seasons he played on the team.

"Jumpin' Joe" Fulks was part of the very first Warriors roster in 1946.

THE ROAD TO GOLDEN STATE

In 1946, in Philadelphia, Pennsylvania, business owner Peter A. Tyrrell founded the Warriors. Tyrrell chose the name to honor a team that had played in the city in the 1920s. The Warriors were one of 11 teams in the Basketball Association of America (BAA).

The Warriors got off to a fast start. Led by their high-scoring forward Joe Fulks, they won the BAA Championship in their first season. Two years later, the BAA joined with another professional basketball league to form the NBA. The Warriors had success in this league as well. They won a second championship in 1956.

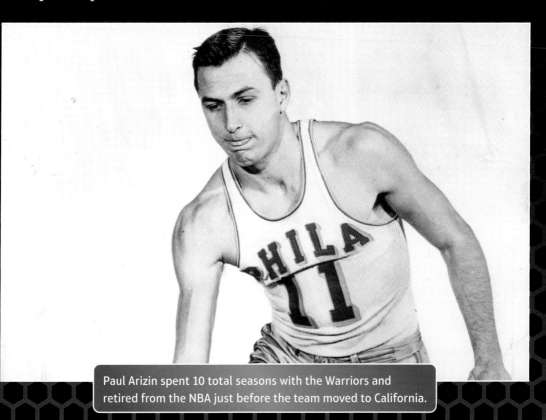

Paul Arizin spent 10 total seasons with the Warriors and retired from the NBA just before the team moved to California.

The Warriors drafted center Wilt Chamberlain in 1959. Standing 7 feet, 1 inch (2.2 m) tall, Wilt the Stilt towered over the other players in the NBA. He quickly showed he was basketball's best scoring center.

The future looked bright for the Warriors, but their time in Philadelphia was over. In 1962, the team moved to California and became the San Francisco Warriors. They played their home games in Oakland and San Jose. They also joined the NBA's Western Division.

The Warriors played home games at Cow Palace in Daly City, California, for seven seasons.

WARRIORS FACT

The team's nickname is the Dubs. Dub is short for the letter *W* in Warriors.

Wilt Chamberlain (*top*) was the NBA's scoring leader seven times in his career.

Wilt Chamberlain continued to score and set records. In 1964, the Warriors made it to the NBA Finals. But they lost to the Boston Celtics in five games. Then, the Warriors' owners traded Chamberlain to the Philadelphia 76ers in 1965.

Rick Barry averaged 25.7 points per game and won the NBA Rookie of the Year award in his first season with the Warriors.

The Warriors began to build a new team around new draft picks Nate Thurmond and Rick Barry. The team owners decided they needed a new name with their new roster. California is nicknamed the Golden State. In 1971, the team became the Golden State Warriors.

Nate Thurmond was the first NBA player to record a quadruple-double in a game with 22 points, 14 rebounds, 13 assists, and 12 blocked shots.

Don "Nellie" Nelson coached the Warriors from 1988 to 1995 and 2006 to 2010. He is widely considered one of the NBA's greatest coaches of all time.

GREATEST MOMENTS

The Warriors made history from the start when they beat the Chicago Stags in five games to win the first ever BAA Championship in 1947. Two seasons later, Joe Fulks scored 63 points in one game. That was the most points per game in NBA history at the time. That record lasted 10 years. Fulks was one of four early Warriors to make the Basketball Hall of Fame. The others were Paul Arizin, Neil Johnston, and Tom Gola. They helped win the team's second championship in 1956.

One of the greatest college athletes of all time, Tom Gola brought his skill to the Warriors and won a championship in his rookie year.

In 1962, Wilt Chamberlain set a record by scoring 100 points in a single game against the New York Knicks. This NBA record still stands. After trading away Chamberlain, the Warriors played in different arenas and different California cities from San Jose to San Diego. They finally settled in the Oakland Arena in 1971. Four years later, the team beat the Washington Bullets in the NBA Finals. The Warriors' victory was one of the biggest Finals upsets in NBA history. It was also the last time they made the Finals for 40 years.

In the 1980s, the Warriors played a style of basketball called Nellie Ball. It was named after their coach Don "Nellie" Nelson. The guards ran fast to get the ball to the basket before the defense could stop them. During a game in 1987, Warriors guard Eric Augustus "Sleepy" Floyd set NBA playoff records by scoring 29 points in a quarter and 39 points in a half. He scored 51 points overall. Nellie Ball worked!

Wilt Chamberlain's 100-point single game record is unlikely to be broken by another player.

The Warriors drafted point guard Stephen Curry in 2009. Curry was a strong shooter and a master of the three-point shot. In his fourth season, Curry scored 54 points in one game at Madison Square Garden in New York City. The amazing performance showed he was the NBA's newest superstar.

It took a while to build a strong team around Curry. But in 2015, the Warriors beat the Cleveland Cavaliers to win the NBA Finals in six games.

The Warriors showed they were one of the greatest teams in NBA history with their titles in 2017, 2018, and 2022. Fans are excited to see how many championship banners they will add to their collection.

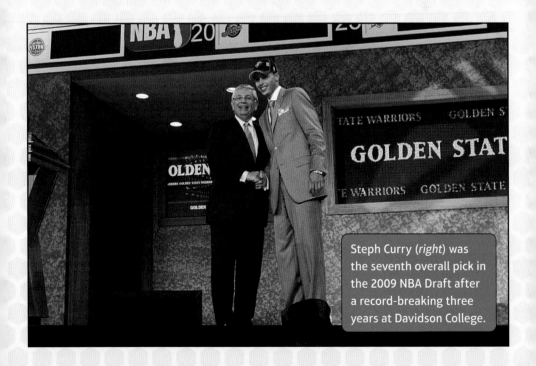

Steph Curry (*right*) was the seventh overall pick in the 2009 NBA Draft after a record-breaking three years at Davidson College.

Steph Curry has set his own record for three-pointers made in a season three times.

WARRIORS SUPERSTARS

Hall of Famer Joe Fulks was the first of many superstar Warriors. Fulks played for the Warriors from their start in 1946 until 1954. Fans called him Jumpin' Joe because of his amazing jump shots. Fulks averaged 23.2 points per game in his first year with the Warriors. That made him the scoring champion for the 1946–1947 NBA season.

Joe Fulks (*left*) and Paul Arizin (*right*) were the Warriors' top scorers for the 1950–1951 and 1951–1952 seasons.

Many people say that Wilt Chamberlain was the greatest Warrior of all, even though he only spent five and a half seasons with the team. Chamberlain averaged 41.5 points per game with the Warriors. Some said that he could dunk by jumping from the free-throw line. That's 15 feet (4.6 m) away from the basket!

After the team traded Chamberlain, the Warriors built their team around two new stars. Forward Nate Thurmond was one of the best rebounders in NBA history. He had five seasons with more than 18 rebounds per game. Thurmond's rebounds set up shots for guard Rick Barry. Barry scored more than 18,000 points in his NBA career. Barry also led the league in steals during the 1974–1975 season.

Chris Mullin averaged 25 or more points per game for five straight seasons with the Warriors, from 1988 to 89 until 1992 to 93.

Stephen Curry is the greatest three-point shooter in NBA history. He scored a record-breaking 402 three-pointers in the 2015–2016 season! That year, Curry won the NBA MVP award for the second time in a row.

Tim Hardaway Sr. was a three-time All-Star during his seven seasons with the Warriors.

In the 1980s, the Warriors looked to three stars to lead them to the top of the Western Conference. Tim Hardaway, Mitch Richmond, and Chris Mullin all liked to run down the court and shoot from long distances. Fans called the three players Run TMC.

Klay Thompson is a four-time NBA champion and a one-time Olympic gold medalist.

But these three never won a championship with the Warriors. Golden State didn't win another title until guards Stephen Curry and Klay Thompson joined the team. They were nicknamed the Splash Brothers because their shots splashed into the basket. Curry liked to score from long distances. When defenders ganged up on him, he passed the ball to Thompson. Thompson always seemed to score three-pointers when the team needed them.

In 2016, the Warriors signed Kevin Durant to join Curry and Thompson. Durant was an All-Star forward. He added even more scoring to the Warriors offense. At 6 feet 10 inches (2.1 m) tall, Durant could score from anywhere on the court. His strong defense helped the Warriors stop opponents in close games. Durant was the Finals MVP two years in a row. He helped the Warriors top LeBron James and the Cleveland Cavaliers to complete their back-to-back championships.

Kevin Durant (*left*) speeds past James Harden (*right*) in a 2019 game between the Warriors and the Houston Rockets.

BACK ON TOP

In 2019, the Warriors lost the NBA Finals to the Toronto Raptors. Golden State did not get their third straight title. After the season, Kevin Durant left the team to join the Brooklyn Nets. Klay Thompson had leg injuries that kept him off the court for two seasons.

The team refused to give up. The Warriors moved across the bay from Oakland to San Francisco in the fall of 2019. They opened the new Chase Center arena in San Francisco. With Durant gone and Thompson injured, the team focused on drafting new players. The Warriors selected center James Wiseman number two overall in the 2020 NBA Draft. They also received forward Andrew Wiggins in a trade. These talented newcomers helped the team begin a new chase for a championship.

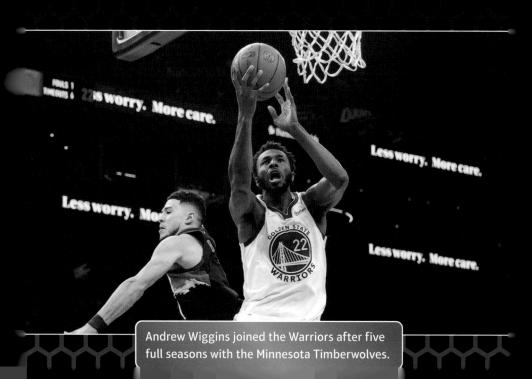

Andrew Wiggins joined the Warriors after five full seasons with the Minnesota Timberwolves.

In 2021, the Warriors were one of the best teams in the NBA once again. On December 14, 2021, in a game against the New York Knicks at Madison Square Garden, Curry scored a three-pointer from 28 feet (8.5 m). This three-pointer made him the NBA's all-time leader in three-point shots. The Warriors called a time-out so that Curry could celebrate his record-breaking three-pointer in front of the cheering crowd.

Later that season, Thompson returned to the court. The Splash Brothers were back! Thompson and Curry led the Warriors to the 2022 NBA Finals. They beat the Boston Celtics in six games. The Warriors had won their fourth championship since 2015. With the Splash Brothers leading the way, Warriors fans expect more championships to come.

Klay Thompson (*center*) wasted no time returning to his former level of play, scoring 17 points in his first game back on the court and averaging 19.3 points per game for the rest of the 2021–2022 season.

Steph Curry was named the NBA Finals MVP for the first time in his career in 2022.

Manute Bol only spent three seasons with the Warriors, but he ranks fifth in team history with 592 blocked shots.

WARRIORS
SEASON RECORD
HOLDERS

POINTS

1. Wilt Chamberlain, 4,029 (1961–1962)
2. Wilt Chamberlain, 3,586 (1962–1963)
3. Wilt Chamberlain, 3,033 (1960–1961)
4. Wilt Chamberlain, 2,948 (1963–1964)
5. Rick Barry, 2,775 (1966–1967)

ASSISTS

1. Sleepy Floyd, 848 (1986–1987)
2. Guy Rodgers, 846 (1965–1966)
3. Guy Rodgers, 825 (1962–1963)
4. Tim Hardaway, 807 (1991–1992)
5. Tim Hardaway, 793 (1990–1991)

REBOUNDS

1. Wilt Chamberlain, 2,149 (1960–1961)
2. Wilt Chamberlain, 2,052 (1961–1962)
3. Wilt Chamberlain, 1,946 (1962–1963)
4. Wilt Chamberlain, 1,941 (1959–1960)
5. Wilt Chamberlain, 1,787 (1963–1964)

BLOCKED SHOTS

1. Manute Bol, 345 (1988–1989)
2. Manute Bol, 238 (1989–1990)
3. Robert Parish, 217 (1978–1979)
4. Adonal Foyle, 205 (2002–2003)
5. Nate Thurmond, 179 (1973–1974)

STEALS

1. Rick Barry, 228 (1974–1975)
2. Tim Hardaway, 214 (1990–1991)
3. Rick Barry, 202 (1975–1976)
4. Baron Davis, 191 (2007–2008)
5. Latrell Sprewell, 180 (1993–1994)

THREE-POINT BASKETS

1. Stephen Curry, 402 (2015–2016)
2. Stephen Curry, 354 (2018–2019)
3. Stephen Curry, 337 (2020–2021)
4. Stephen Curry, 324 (2016–2017)
5. Stephen Curry, 286 (2014–2015)

GLOSSARY

assist: a pass that leads directly to a score

center: a tall player who usually plays near the basket and the center of the court

draft: when teams take turns choosing new players

dunk: a shot in basketball made by jumping high into the air and throwing the ball down through the basket

forward: a player who usually plays near the basket

guard: a basketball player who usually plays in the backcourt

jump shot: a shot in basketball made by jumping into the air and releasing the ball with one or both hands at the peak of the jump

rebound: catching a basketball after a missed shot

triple-double: when a player reaches at least 10 in three different stats categories in a game

LEARN MORE

Golden State Warriors
https://www.nba.com/warriors/

Jr. NBA
https://jr.nba.com/

Kelley, K. C. *Golden State Warriors*. Mankato, MN: Child's World, 2019.

Levit, Joe. *Meet Stephen Curry*. Minneapolis: Lerner Publications, 2023.

Sports Illustrated Kids—Basketball
https://www.sikids.com/basketball

Walker, Hubert. *Stephen Curry: Basketball Star*. Lake Elmo, MN: North Star Editions, 2021.

INDEX

PHOTO ACKNOWLEDGMENTS

Image credits: Gregory Shamus/Staff/Getty Images, p.4; Jason Miller/ Stringer/Getty Images, p.6; Gregory Shamus/Staff/Getty Images, p.7; Halvorsen brian/Wikimedia, p.8; Staff/MCT/Newscom, p.9; Joseph Sohm/ Shutterstock, p.10; Halvorsen brian/Wikimedia, p.11; Halvorsen brian/ Wikimedia, p.12; Halvorsen brian/Wikimedia, p.13; Otto Greule Jr/ Stringer/Getty Images, p.14; Halvorsen brian/Wikimedia, p.15; Chris Szagola/Cal Sport Media/Newscom, p.16; Jim McIsaac/Staff/Getty Images, p.17; Ezra Shaw/Staff/Getty Images, p.18; Halvorsen brian/Wikimedia, p.19; Tim DeFrisco/Stringer/Getty Images, p.20; Mike Powell/Staff/ Getty Images, p.21; Ezra Shaw/Staff/Getty Images, p.22; Tim Warner/ Stringer/Getty Images, p.23; Ezra Shaw/Staff/Getty Images, 24; Christian Petersen/Staff/Getty Images, p.25; Thearon W. Henderson/Stringer/Getty Images, p.26; Al Bello/Staff/Getty Images, p.27; Mike Powell/Staff/Getty Images, p.28

Design element: Master3D/Shutterstock.com.

Cover image: Sean Gardner/Stringer/Getty Images